I0017237

Marketing For The Internet Age

New Revised Edition

Hello. Thank you for checking out our eBook. If you liked the information in this booklet or would like to support The Modern Time, please subscribe to our blog at the link below. Every sub counts.

https://themoderntime.com

Introduction

There has been a rapid increase in internet usage worldwide every day. It is estimated that over four billion people worldwide have access to the internet. Marketing has always existed, and it involves reaching customers in the locations where they are. TV commercials, print advertisements, and billboards have been attempting to do this for decades.

Using the internet for marketing has numerous benefits beyond being a medium for exchanging information. The benefits include a broader audience, personalized content, and the ability to establish a far-reaching rapport with customers, among many others.

In modern times, the internet has evolved beyond being just a means to access information on the go; it has also become a vital tool for many businesses to reach their target audiences.

According to a survey conducted by SmartInsights with over 600 participants who were mostly digital marketing managers or executives, approximately 34% of those businesses had internet marketing integrated into their overall marketing strategies. The same report found that 49% of participants used digital marketing but did not have a strategic plan in place for their campaigns.

This data gives us an idea of just how many businesses use digital marketing as a fundamental part of their operations. In a rapidly expanding technological society, it is essential to keep up with the latest trends to reach customers and clients effectively.

By understanding basic concepts of internet marketing along with newer applications, we can effectively increase our leads and heighten our potential revenue.

In this booklet, I will introduce you to some of the most effective tools for marketing in the internet age.

Marketing

Marketing, simply put, is the promotion of goods and services for sale or purchase. A marketing agent is someone who facilitates the promotion of goods or services for buying or selling. As a marketer, it is your responsibility to connect potential buyers with their needs.

Many marketers work for other companies to expand their customer base or boost the sales of their products or services. Today's marketing specialists may use a wide range of tools and options to reach their target audiences. Blogs, digital magazines, infographics, and podcasts are just a few examples of ways that businesses can market their products and services.

Businesses may also leverage analytics and other data to learn their customers' specific wants or needs, often before they are realized. Businesses must be continually willing to embrace new developments in technology and reassess their overall strategies to align with evolving customer demands.

Recognizing potential weaknesses in marketing campaign strategies and growing market competition is vital for success in developing effective conversions. Utilizing a series of platforms and other internet options a business can market themselves to the world in real-time. Identifying a target audience can be simple as narrowing in on a specific demographic or subset of people who are the most likely to be customers or clients.

Zeroing in on your target audience is imperative for effective marketing and communication strategies. It helps tailor messages, content, and advertising to resonate with the preferences, needs, and interests of that specific group. Factors such as age, gender, location, income level, interests, lifestyle, and purchasing behavior are commonly considered when defining a target audience. After identifying who is most likely to need what you are offering, you are ready to begin marketing your services to the world.

Now, I will give you a few fundamental examples of today's latest internet marketing methods as well as various platforms that have generated incredible success for many of today's budding and established entrepreneurs.

Examples of Internet Marketing

1. Blog Posts

A blog is an online platform that provides users a space to organize their posts, web pages, and all the content that will be featured on their website or URL. Your blog posts act as branches that extend to all corners of the internet and search engines, while the blog itself is like a tree trunk.

When users access these links, they will be directed back to your site, thereby increasing your potential leads and sales over time. A blog can be an invaluable asset for businesses seeking to connect with their audience in a more personal and engaging manner.

A great blog will also help you attract loyal customers, fans, and followers. With subscription options available to your visitors, your blog subscribers can be regularly updated on changes that are taking place, events and promotions that are being held by your business or its affiliates.

Blogs help to build authority, demonstrate expertise, provide valuable insight, drive traffic, and increase conversion opportunities.

2. Infographics

Infographics are a visual and attractive way to present information or data to your audiences. By utilizing a combination of images, charts, graphs, and text, you can effectively present even the most intricate ideas or concepts in a clear and easily understandable format.

The contents that are created using infographics are easy to digest & can be shared quickly across a large spectrum in rapid succession.

3. Case studies

A case study is another popular and useful strategy for building customer trust. This is an in-depth analysis of the actions that have led to success for your brand or business. It can be any achievement you have accomplished for your clients. Case studies are valuable for marketing and promotion because they provide real-world examples of how a company can positively impact its clients.

Credibility and trust are enhanced when prospective clients learn about the positive experience's others have had while doing business with your company. They can observe how the products or services of the business are used in real-life, often in relatable scenarios. They can also assess whether they will receive the expected outcome or benefit based on previous performance metrics.

4. Podcasts

Crafting a blog post can be challenging for some individuals, as it demands specific skills and effort, including website management and consistent creation of long-form content.

However, another option is podcasts, which may be beneficial for those who struggle with writing. It is to narrate stories through audio or broadcasting a message on a digital radio station that people can also download and listen to past episodes later.

This type of content will work well if you are a skilled interviewer or if your public speaking skills are top-notch. Today, podcasts are widely popular and have grown many businesses into successful endeavors.

Podcasts give their audiences the ability to listen without giving all their attention to one task, making it easy to digest the information without sacrificing their entire focus. It can also be a very effective and often times entertaining way to build relationships with the people who patronize your services.

5. Videos / Reels

Video content has quickly grown to become one of the most popular forms of content in today's internet society. There are numerous reasons why videos are popular.

Videos are highly engaging compared to other forms of content, such as text or images. They can captivate viewers with movement, sound, and visuals, keeping their attention and offering entertainment.

They offer users a dynamic way of being informed and do not require as much effort as reading articles or blog posts.

Thanks to today's social media trends, short-form videos, typically 60 seconds or less, provide viewers with the ability to grasp concepts quickly and effectively without sacrificing much time, making them a convenient option for busy audiences.

Videos can bring forth emotions in a way that words or pictures alone cannot. Build an emotional connection with viewers by integrating music, narratives, and visuals to evoke feelings of inspiration, enthusiasm, or empathy.

Now we will discuss several types of Internet Marketing that all marketers in the internet age should become familiar with.

Types of Internet Marketing

1. **Social media marketing** refers to grabbing customers' attention and capturing sales through social media platforms such as Facebook, Instagram, and Twitter.

   Today, social media has been used at least once by nearly 3/4ths of the world population. This makes social media one of the most effective tools for reaching a wide range of different people in your target audience.

   Social media platforms also come with a variety of options that allow businesses to operate multiple strategies in one domain. It can further be divided into two subgroups that include;

[1]Organic Social Media Marketing

Organic social media marketing refers to promoting a brand, product, or service through non-paid methods on social media platforms. It allows businesses to build a community that will deepen the relationship with its clients while striving to achieve customer loyalty.

Increasing brand awareness without relying on paid advertising or promotions is the basis of organic social marketing.

[2]Paid social media marketing

Paid social media marketing is using social media networks to advertise a company, product, or service. This usually refers to paid promotional content that is targeted to specific demographics, interests, or behaviors, such as sponsored posts, display advertisements, video ads, and other similar content.

With paid social media marketing, companies may invest money to expand the reach and efficacy of their campaigns, reach a wider audience, build brand awareness, drive website traffic, and produce leads or sales. You can pay, for example, Facebook, to promote existing organic posts. They are known as Pay Per click or Pay Per View.

3. Search Engine Optimization

Search engine optimization involves optimizing websites and digital content to improve their search engine rankings. The improved search rankings will ensure your website attracts more new visitors. There are two sub-types of search engine optimization that includes;

[1]**Off-page SEO** which involves the optimization of a website or other content to enable it to appear higher in search rankings using the method outside the website or content location.

[2]**On-page SEO** involves optimizing a website or other content to rank higher in search engines using specifically targeted keywords or phrases.

4. Content marketing

Content marketing refers to the creation, distribution, and promotion of relevant online materials so that it gets attention that creates engagement to convert the target market into customers. Content today is one of the most widely talked about subjects for online businesses.

Using various social media platforms, businesses are working to develop attractive, visual representations of the products or services they provide to reach millions of active users and potential customers.

5. Influencer marketing

An influencer is a person with a substantial social media following. Influencer marketing is working with these people to promote your products on their social media platforms. By partnering with influencers, you can build customer trust while reaching extended audiences.

Paying careful attention to which influencers offer the best potential for your brand is vital to influencer marketing. Ensuring they have the appropriate audience can determine if they can be effective in helping you reach your marketing goals.

6.Affiliate marketing

Affiliate marketing involves paying people that own external websites or other traffic networks a commission for the traffic or sales they make for your brand. By creating affiliate partnerships, you can begin to earn more while also helping other entrepreneurs expand their product catalog.

E-commerce sites like Amazon have become one of the most popular affiliate marketing programs to date. They pay their affiliates a varying percentage of referred sales based on item type. Many people have even made a living through affiliate programs by referring products that are offered by already established businesses.

Note: Each business can be categorized into a specific niche. For building an effective and high-quality marketing strategy, you will have to focus on a specific group of people who are expected to use your services or purchase your products. Putting up random advertisements on multiple platforms is more than likely to yield results that drift below your marketing potential. It has been proven time again that directing your marketing efforts towards a narrowed group of potential customers is much better than generalized promotion.

11 Methods to boost leads

By using one or a combination of the following methods you can potentially increase your lead generation tenfold. Try making introductory videos to get your message out.

1. **Social media**

Social media platforms have over 300 million active users every hour. It is easy to see why it would be the first on our list.

With the most popular platforms generating multi-billion-dollar annual revenues, largely from millions of ad users, social media platforms like Facebook and X (formerly Twitter) can quickly become a network filled with potential clients.

Even with a small budget of only $20, an otherwise unnoticed campaign can quickly generate hundreds or thousands of potential connections. Quality ad targeting methods will enable you to reach the individuals most likely to be interested in your offering, so be sure to research the optimal keywords for your specific product.

Always provide a means for viewers to connect with you outside of their specific platforms. Stories have grown to become one of the most popular aspects of social networking. Utilizing stories to capture your follower's attention may even prove to be one of your most effective marketing tactics later.

By using Facebook groups, you can actively expand your network beyond the people you already know. Join Facebook groups with a specific focus. Do not, for example, join Dream Cars Worldwide with the intention of selling car parts because the group's purpose is too broad. Look for a local or regional group of car enthusiasts, as they are more likely to attract serious buyers.

Avoid joining groups that have an excessive amount of irrelevant and frequent posts, as your message may be overlooked as spam.

2. Classifieds

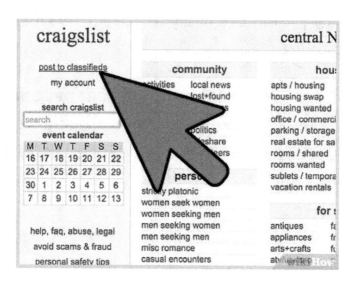

On average, thousands of people view a dozen classified ads every day. Have you ever browsed Craigslist for a vehicle or an apartment? How many items did you view before finding something you liked? The point is that almost anyone with a classified ad will receive views.

` By posting a high-quality ad on various

platforms such as Craigslist, eBay classifieds, or Yahoo, you can effectively reach hundreds of additional leads over time.

Always keep your ads updated for the best results and explore smaller pages that have local users who may benefit from your services.

When using classifieds remember, you can be everywhere at one time. Think Universal.

3. Digital Flyers

One of the most powerful tools for marketing in the internet age is having a captivating digital flyer. A successful flyer will feature a striking image and a very catchy headline that captures the customer's attention.

You can include information about the product or services you provide, pricing, contact information, address, or website. Please ensure that you include any additional information that will help readers understand what you are offering.

4. Keep practicing different marketing strategies until you find one that works for you, and you will become successful. Always think Universal. If you could, how would you reach everyone regardless of where they are?

5. Message Boards

Message boards, also known as bulletin boards or forums, are one of the earliest forms of online social networks, dating back to the early 1990s when the internet first gained widespread popularity.

Today, with the evolution of social media networks such as Facebook and Myspace, message boards almost seem like ancient fossils. However, thousands of message boards still exist today and are being used for communication, information exchange, and networking on a global scale.

Message boards are communities of people, both small and large, who share common interests. If you want to build a solid network, one of the most effective ways to do so is by being an active contributor to a forum focused on a particular niche.

6.Mailing list

A mailing list, sometimes referred to as a newsletter, is a compilation of individuals who have consented to receive your updates via mail. Many people want to be the first to know when something becomes available.

By creating a mailing list and allowing others to subscribe via email, you can send information about your products or services, as well as deals and promotions, to people who are eagerly awaiting them.

An email list lets you stay in touch with many people without having to send individual messages to each person. It is important to send only high-quality emails at regular intervals to avoid being flagged as spam by the email filter system.

7.SMS ALERTS

Today SMS alerts are one of the most convenient ways for businesses to keep customers updated on the latest information on news, products, and services. By providing their mobile number, you will be able to stay connected with your customers. SMS alerts allow you to send out mass messages to all your clients at once.

TextMate and Clicksend are great starting points if you need something setup right away. Just be sure to deliver a concise message campaign that is as short as possible, while limiting the number of daily messages to avoid losing subscribers or being reported for spam.

8. Discord / Telegram

Discord and Telegram have opened the doorway for many to build their own community and to remain active with their most loyal customers or fan base. They both enable users to chat, join communities, and with Discord, you can even play various games together.

Discord allows you to host live broadcasts and video conferences, use VOIP features, create various chatrooms based on specific topics or categories and much more. They also offer many premium features that allow users the opportunity to contribute and donate to the overall success of your community.

Discord may be a tool you want to use if you value the cultivating of community-based operations within your company or brand strategy.

9. Direct message or conversation

One of the most effective ways to connect with potential clients is by having a direct conversation about the products or services you offer. The direct approach allows you to introduce yourself on a one-on-one basis while giving you the added advantage of building the confidence of both you and the customer.

Next time you want to market your product try introducing yourself through the direct approach. Sending direct messages through various internet portals, introducing yourself and then getting to know your customers can have a massive impact on your success and even help to get the word out about your brand or business.

10.   YouTube

There are now thousands of YouTubers making a decent amount of money by recording their own videos. YouTube quickly grew to become the most successful video sharing platform worldwide, with millions of videos being uploaded and billions of hours being watched daily.

Growing a YouTube channel that

offers interesting or informative content can become a profitable endeavor, especially for marketing your business. Many people also use YouTube to teach others how to do things they are good at or simply to keep people informed about various subjects. YouTube can help build an audience that converts viewers into customers.

11.   Reddit

Reddit is a giant online bulletin board where people from all over the world can share and discuss nearly anything you can think of. Users post links, text, images, or videos on specific topics in "subreddits," which are akin to distinct rooms or communities dedicated to various interests.

Reddit is known for its diverse user base and discussions. Marketing your products or services through various Reddit channels may prove to be one of the most effective tools in your arsenal. Make sure to post often and do not be afraid to use different subreddits to get your message out.

That is 11 Marketing methods to boost your leads. No matter what business you are in, with the right effort you can grow your customer base.

Try applying the 11 methods in this book using a mix of photo and video content on various platforms across the web and be sure to tell us how it went!

SEO

Now, we will discuss seven search engine optimization methods that will enhance your search engine ranking. Search engine optimization helps increase your likelihood of appearing at the top of search engine results.

Search engines such as Google, Yahoo, and MSN rely on keywords and phrases to rank pages. Pages that are most relevant to the search terms receive the highest rating and are displayed first.

With proper search engine optimization, your website can rank higher in search results. Your page will appear in the top search results, driving traffic to your website.

Importance of SEO

Why is SEO important?

With search engine optimization, web pages that best represent a person's desired information become visible at the top of their search engine results.

If you own a business called Pete's Vegetables, it is important that when people search for your business on Google, it appears in the top three search results. Several factors may come into play that can influence this. Factors such as the prevalence of other businesses with the same name having a strong online presence.

The more unique the name or the stronger the presence, the more likely it is to rank number one on most search engines. A strong online presence is achieved by having high-quality web pages that effectively define the purpose of the website.

Now that we know the importance of search engine optimization, let us go over 7 methods to optimize our pages.

If you're unsure about how to optimize your website or social media for search engines, contact admin@themoderntime.com to inquire about SEO services

1. Keywords

If there was any tool for a web page that could singlehandedly win a search engine's attention, it would have to be keywords. Keywords which are defined as

a significant word from a title or document u sed especially as an index to content

Keywords are essential for search engine optimization. In fact, most search engines act like scavengers, constantly scouring the Internet for keywords. With keywords, search engines can not only determine how frequently a site uses certain words and phrases, but also how consistent a site is at staying true to its purpose.

Using the correct keywords is vital when optimizing your website for search engines. It is important to be consistent in forming words and phrases that accurately describe your product, service, or business.

Never miss the opportunity to incorporate the name of your business, product, or service into as many of your web pages, blogs, or news articles as possible, without making it appear cluttered or off-topic.

2. Meta Data

Although believed by many to be an ancient concept, metadata, which consists of invisible lines of code that headline web pages and are usually recognized by scripts, helps improve your search engine optimization results.

Scripts, which are programs run by other web pages, use metadata to help them recognize the type of pages from which they are acquiring data. This helps them quickly categorize a page based on its intended purpose. Without metadata, scripts may sometimes incorrectly categorize a web page, leading to poor SEO.

3. Image Attributes

Have you ever gone to Google and done an image search? Do you ever wonder how Google finds millions of images? The answer is image attributes. Image attributes, simply put, are pieces of information that describe an image. A special code is required to display this information.

```
<img src="image.jpg" alt="image
description" title="image title"
```

Users of blogging platforms like WordPress will find it easy to upload an image and add details such as title, alternative text, and image description in the provided boxes within the media upload tool.

By using image attributes, people can discover your page when searching for images related to their search results. Always remember to include image attributes.

4. Back Links

Backlinking is the process of linking one website to another. Backlinking allows people who are visiting other websites the opportunity to discover your content. Since search engines are constantly crawling the web in search of content to archive, these backlinks provide a significant advantage.

When a person searches for your website or related content, the likelihood of them finding your page compared to others will increase with the proper use of backlinks. Think of it as having endorsements. Placing your link in various locations on the internet can enhance your overall visibility and influence search results, providing an advantage in achieving higher rankings.

Quality backlinking involves identifying websites that are relevant to your content and creating a link back to your website, either through comments on blog posts, partnership opportunities, or other methods.

Try reaching out to websites that are in your niche and asking them if they will allow you to post relevant content on their site. Remember to include a link back to your own channels or website to establish domain authority.

5. Cache Cleanup

A cache is a feature that stores certain elements of a page on a virtual disk to help websites load faster. It is important to consistently monitor your cache usage if your website utilizes this feature and to clear your cache whenever you make changes to a web page. By doing so, you ensure that your visitors, including search crawlers, receive the most current version of your website, rather than a previously cached copy. This will also benefit your results in the search engines by making sure that they have the most updated version of your page. For this reason, clearing your cache is an important step to search engine optimization.

6. Quality Content

One of the most important rules for ranking on search engines is to offer high-quality pages that are easy to categorize. Ensure that your metadata, keywords, and any images or videos focus on a single topic and are easy to comprehend.

Avoid using excessive words or phrases that are not direct or to the point, as this can negatively impact search engine results. Keywords determine search result rankings. You don't want to appear as a seafood restaurant blog on Google when you're actually a fishing page.

7. Consistency

The last, but also the most powerful, tool for search engine optimization is consistency. As you continue to develop your website, search engines will eventually recognize your progress, leading to higher rankings.

The more high-quality content you produce and the more pages you develop, the larger your presence becomes on the Internet. This, in turn, contributes to your digital footprint or online real estate.

SEO OPTIMIZING FOR SOCIAL MEDIA

Millions of people are using social media to launch, develop and market their business today. You may have just started developing your social media platform and want to know a few tips to help you get more traffic. That is where Social Media Optimization comes into play. A system that employs several strategies and methods to aid you in building an audience through social networks.

WHAT IS SOCIAL MEDIA OPTIMIZATION?

Social media optimization refers to the optimization of a website or its page elements and content to increase awareness, improve viewability and searchability through social media channels. So, what does that mean?

Social media optimization is developing your site to be easy to navigate and appealing to many social media consumers. It is studying and figuring out what elements on your site could potentially be optimized better for social media access.

It is also measuring how an individual product page, piece of content or an email will be shared through social media channels like Facebook or Twitter. By looking at these site elements you are trying to figure out how you might be able to use proper SMO to develop your site to better gain more traffic and conversion.

There are a couple of things that you can do to provide social media optimization for your website.

One of the most common ways that people optimize their sites for social media is by adding sharing buttons to their content. Another is by using attention grabbing headlines that drive engagement and potential conversion or sales.

HOW DOES SOCIAL MEDIA OPTIMIZATION BENEFIT MY WEBSITE?

Using social media allows you to drive traffic conversions and allows you to engage closely with your customers and potential clients.

Social Media Optimization is very similar to SEO in many ways, although there are a few distinct differences. Elements such as keywords and page elements like meta titles, descriptions, H1 & H2 tags all exist through social profiles just like in SEO.

By right-clicking and viewing the source of a social profile using a desktop computer, you will be able to see the page elements allowing you to measure proper keyword placement and optimization techniques in those areas, just as you would with SEO.

The quality of a page is of the utmost importance because it helps search engines to pick up the content. Also, many people who view your page will want to find what they are looking for as well as be able to quickly navigate social elements.

Try not to add too many sharing buttons to an individual page. Driving traffic is the goal, the same with SEO strategies.

When you are optimizing your pages for social media, think about generating more traffic for your site. Having backlinks is also important for overall success. Networks like Twitter allow users to retweet posts which create nofollow links that can be crawled by the search engines. Backlinks help people to find your site faster by providing multiple sources where the content can be traced. Look for opportunities to use SMO and SEO optimization to maximize your pages potential.

HOW TO GET STARTED IN SOCIAL MEDIA OPTIMIZATION?

The best way to get started with Social Media Optimization is to follow the principles of Search Engine Optimization (SEO). Use keywords that best describe what your content is about. Avoid using too many keywords that make it hard to understand what you are presenting.

Look at your website from the viewpoint of the audience and find ways to improve their site experience. Then look for ways to give them more social access. You can do this using third-party tools or adding one-click social login functions like Open Graph so they can sign in directly through their Facebook, Twitter, or Google accounts.

Create a reward system for engagements by thanking them for liking, commenting, sharing, or purchasing from you. Show them that you appreciate their actions, and this will attract more people to your content. The best time to get started on optimizing your site for social media is now.

Analyze your website and your target audience and think about how they will engage with your website through social channels. Provide them with the tools that it takes to create social engagement and always stay on top of new social trends that can benefit you in the future.

To generate traffic for your site and create an audience you are going to need to optimize your site for social media and search engines. If you want to learn more about Social Media Optimization, Search Engine Optimization or other techniques contact us!

Common Mistakes of Internet Marketers

To help you navigate your road to building effective marketing strategies, here are a few common mistakes you want to avoid.

1. **Not Using Data Analytics or Insights**: Analytics help better understand how customers interact with your business or social media platform. It gives you an idea of what is or is not working and how you can adjust your program to reach specific target goals. Failing to analyze and understand data from website traffic, social media engagement, and other metrics can result in ineffective strategies. It is essential to monitor analytics to make informed decisions and optimize marketing efforts.

2. **Focusing Only on Sales**: Constantly pushing sales pitches without providing value or building relationships can alienate potential customers. Successful internet marketers prioritize creating valuable content, engaging with their audience, and building trust before promoting products or services.

3. **Neglecting the Target Audience**: Failing to understand or accurately define the target audience can lead to ineffective messaging and wasted resources. Marketers should conduct comprehensive research to identify the needs, preferences, and behaviors of their ideal customers.

4. **Neglecting SEO**: can hinder a website's visibility and organic traffic. By ignoring search engine optimization (SEO) practices you are making yourself invisible

to user search queries. Marketers should optimize their content by incorporating relevant keywords, meta tags, and high-quality backlinks to enhance their search engine rankings.

5. **Ignoring Feedback**: Failing to monitor and respond to customer feedback, mentions, or inquiries on social media can harm brand reputation and customer relationships. Marketers should actively listen to social conversations and engage with their audience to cultivate trust and loyalty.

By avoiding these common mistakes and staying updated on the latest trends and best practices, internet marketers can improve their strategies and achieve greater success in reaching their goals.

Enjoy creating content and always remember to consult this guide when you need help optimizing your page's search engine results.

For more information on Marketing for the Internet Age visit our website:

themoderntime.com

YOUR AD HERE

Contact us to learn more about advertising your product in our next eBook!

Admin@themoderntime.com

YOU CAN DONATE TO SUPPORT OUR EXPANSION EFFORTS

We appreciate donations of any kind to help us achieve our goals.

Contact editor@themoderntime.com if you would like to donate to support our efforts.

Marketing For The Internet Age, Second Edition.

Publish your Business in The Modern Time for Increased Exposure

Are you an entrepreneur that has an amazing product or service that can use more exposure to the public? Do you have any news or announcements about future products, services, or events? Maybe you are working to innovate and advance the culture, the way we live or do business? We want to publish you on our network.

We are The Modern Time. We aim to inspire the next generation of innovation through resource and information.

Business marketing can be complex. You have a product, or a service and you want more people to know about it. You could just stand in the street and yell about it, but that might not be the best way. You may also post it on your social media page, but that will only reach your immediate friends. Often, they could be the least likely to be interested.

With the number of businesses competing in these arenas, having a more effective option of reaching larger crowds in modern times is mandatory.

News and press releases are one of the best ways to market your business. Though it is one of the oldest methods of marketing, it is still one of the most effective. You could reach many potential clients and control a larger range of market share. But why are press and news articles so effective?

Benefits that press and news articles provide:

• Be Found Through Search Engines (SEO)
• Increased Exposure
• Higher Sales Potential
• Improves Brand Reputation
• Residual Traffic to your Site/Social Media
• Distribute Content to Larger Audience
• Provides Historical References
• Improves Media Relationships
• Become More Attractive to Investors

and much more!

We also offer Advertising space on our website that will allow you to tap into our traffic base to draw potential customers to your website.

To learn more about our Marketing and Advertising services, send us an email to editor@themoderntime.com

We are The Modern Time. A new generation of Innovation.

www.themoderntime.com
A NEW GENERATION OF INNOVATION
BUSINESS | TECH | HEALTH | INNOVATION | RESOURCES

MINORITY BUSINESSES MAY

SUBMIT AN ARTICLE OR PRESS RELEASE

For immediate release to editor@themoderntime.com

GUIDELINES:
Attach a copy of article or press release in DOC or PDF format with relevant pictures in email.
Put in subject line: FOR IMMEDIATE RELEASE
Make sure your article contains at least 300 words or it may be rejected.
Include author name and any relevant links

Accepting
News, Announcements, Promotions, Events, Reviews, Opinions.
Guest bloggers welcome.

We are the Modern Time Information Network.

Mission

Our mission is to advance the next generation of business, technology and innovation through resource and information. We work to develop a network and library of latest news, trends and research from established & upcoming leaders and educators in a vast arena.

We aim to bring the kind of awareness through media that promotes the development of creativity and the furthering of ideas that will evolve the world dynamic for generations to come.

We believe in authoring as well as taking advantage of opportunities that shape and mold our world for the better, while encouraging individuality, originality, and entrepreneurship every step of the way.

We utilize every avenue available to us to reach our audiences and provide them with the type of content that will inspire them to be an active part in leading tomorrow's forefront of a quickly advancing technological society. We will help to take charge of the digital revolution.

Contribute

We are always looking for news, the latest trends and research in business, technology, health and of course innovation. If you want to contribute an article, press release or have any resource you want to add to our site, contact us. You can email us at editor@themoderntime.com

ARE YOU A WRITER OR JOURNALIST?

We are always looking for news, the latest trends and research in business and technology. If you would like to contribute an article or have any resource that you would like to add to our information library please contact us using the form below or you can email us at :

editor@themoderntime.com

THE MODERN

TIME

MODERN INNOVATION MEDIA

INSPIRING THE NEXT GENERATION OF INNOVATION

www.themoderntime.com

ARE YOU 50 OR OLDER?

DID YOU KNOW

THE HUMAN BODY IS **NATURALLY** DESIGNED TO

HEAL
ALL BY ITSELF

DO YOU HAVE A HABIT OF TAKING MEDICATIONS FOR EVERY SIGN OF *DISCOMFORT OR PAIN?*

WHAT IF I TOLD YOU THAT YOUR BODY IS *ALREADY* DESIGNED TO PRODUCE THE **MEDICINE** THAT FIGHTS OFF ANY SICKNESS, DISEASE OR ILLNESS?

WHAT IF I COULD **TEACH** YOU A METHOD TO SPEED UP THE PRO-CESS OF HEALING, FOR NEAR INVINCIBLE HEALTH?

WOULD YOU STILL VISIT THE PHARMACY?

LEARN HOW TO HARNESS THE FULL POTENTIAL OF YOUR BODIES NATURAL ABILITY TO HEAL ITSELF TODAY!

themoderntime.com/seanali

BLACK AUTHOR WITH OVER A DOZEN BOOKS
TEACHING THE ART OF SELF HEALING

INSPIRED BY HOW TO EAT TO LIVE

https://themoderntime.com/seanali

Justice is the founder of The Modern Company, a new generation of innovation. He is also a content writer, researcher, marketer and editor for The Modern Time, a website providing the latest news, resources, and information in the growing world of Business, Technology, Health, and Innovation.